"Pat Egan Dexter has written a series of prayer services making classic Christian meditation accessible to today's middle-grade students. The rituals she shares in this book bring together, in Christ-centered reflections, scripture, familiar objects, and the imagination of the children. She manages to avoid being either excessively abstract or oppressively emotional.

"Even teachers uncertain about meditation or contemplative prayer will find that these exercises lead into natural, nurturing meditative prayers. A wonderful supplement to any kind of religious education program."

Sally Wilkins
Grade School Teacher
Amherst, NH

"The children in our classrooms come from varied family backgrounds, and have so many pressures all around them. It is indeed a gift for a catechist to have an age-appropriate resource to help these children be quiet for awhile, to reflect on the scriptures, and to find within themselves the depths of God's love and the abundance of God's gifts."

Pat Maza
Coordinator, Religious Education
Tempe, AZ

"Pat Dexter has done a wonderful job creating these guided prayer services for middle graders. The correlation of the topics with scripture is wonderful. The strong use of symbols and ritual appeals to children as does the opportunity to be a reader.

"The guided meditations are very creative and challenge the children to use their imaginations. The many invitations for personal sharing, the discussions, and the closing prayers will help the children to grow spiritually and to strengthen their relationship with the Lord and one another.

"I'm very happy to recommend this book to all those who work with middle-grade children."

Marie Tropiano
Director of Catechetical Ministry
St. Timothy Catholic Community
Mesa, AZ

"Middle schoolers are bombarded each day with fast-moving media, which discourages reflective thinking. With *25 Guided Prayer Services for Middle Graders*, teachers can introduce children to concepts not often approached by middle schoolers in a way that fosters reflection. Through the use of personal guided meditations, topics such as counsel, perseverance, wisdom, and covenant are explained and can be incorporated into their life experiences.

"Pat Dexter's book introduces Jesus to children in a way that is both personal and powerful. It is an excellent way to expose students to a wide variety of scripture, and its easy-to-use format makes it a good choice for busy teachers. These guided meditations will help enlarge the students' view of life and give them the spiritual tools to better live it."

Anne E. Neuberger
Columnist, *Religion Teacher's Journal*

"Pat Dexter offers a thought-provoking resource to catechists of middle graders on how to use the Bible and to pray with children. Focusing on twenty-five gifts children have received from God, the guided meditations offer a variety of reflections, some well suited to the seasons and feasts of the church year, as well as to an ordinary day. The gifts reflect the common, everyday world of children, such as hands, friends, rocks, and darkness, together with religious experiences of forgiveness, trust, healing, and prayer.

"Some meditations, like the one on the cross, can be effectively used during Lent, on Good Friday, and feasts of the cross. Others, like the gift of animals or the heart, can be repeated at any time of the year.

"If parents are first introduced to the guided meditation process, they could use the scripture readings and closing prayer with their children as in-home follow-up. What a richness this would add to parent-child prayer and religious formation!"

George Matanic, O.P.
Newman Center
University of Arizona

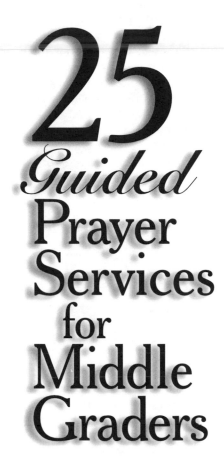

25 Guided Prayer Services for Middle Graders

PAT EGAN DEXTER

TWENTY-THIRD PUBLICATIONS

Mystic, CT 06355

Second printing 1997

Twenty-Third Publications
185 Willow Street
P.O. Box 180
Mystic, CT 06355
(860) 536-2611
800-321-0411

ISBN 0-89622-688-3
Library of Congress Catalog Card Number 95-62342
Printed in the U.S.A.

Dedication

This book is dedicated to my grandchildren:

Michelle Richards

Jacob Koty

Brianna Koty

Charis Dexter

Brian Koty

Grant Dexter

and any grandchild not yet born.

Contents

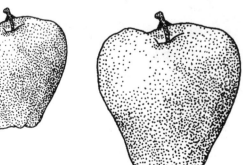

Introduction

One day I was teaching religion to junior-high students at Holy Spirit Church in Tempe, Arizona, when Father Frank knocked on the door. He had come for a visit.

"What are you learning today?" he asked the students.

"Bible stories," came the response.

Father Frank picked up the Bible from my desk, and grinning at my students, he asked, "How about you teaching me?" Silence.

Undaunted, he opened the Bible to Ecclesiastes (3:22).

"Then I saw there is nothing better for people than to rejoice in their work; for this is their lot."

"Now what do *you* think this means?"

Hands sky-rocketed. One student answered, "You might as well have a good attitude about your work because you have to do it anyhow."

Fr. Frank nodded. "Okay, how about this reading from Luke (6:39)."

"Can someone who is blind be a guide to another blind person?"

Again hands raised and waved.

On and on this went for the rest of the class. My students were amazed at how much they already knew about the Bible and how it could be applied to their lives here and now.

Before leaving, Father Frank told them, "The Bible is more than history, more than poetry, more than great stories. It is the continuing story of God's love for us. Continuing! Then. Now. In the future. Forever, like God's relationship with us. The Bible can help you to live a better life, and to have a better relationship with God, and it can be a great map on your journey to God."

Yes! These were my sentiments exactly. I wanted to help my students learn to love the Bible and to open their minds and hearts to its message. I hope I did that in my classes. And now I hope to continue my religious education ministry through this book, which is meant to help other catechists, especially those who teach middle graders, to use the Bible and to pray with their classes.

What's In This Book

Each of these 25 services highlights one of the many gifts children have received from God: gifts of nature, talents, virtues, etc., and begins with scripture readings on that topic. These are followed by a hands-on activity that invites children to see, touch, and reflect on one of these gifts. The heart of each service is a guided meditation that leads children into an experience of prayer and reflection. Finally, there is a closing prayer that involves the entire group.

These services would work well in a variety of settings. First and most obviously, catechists and teachers will find them helpful for beginning or ending their religion classes. They are also appropriate for mini-retreats or special seasonal programs during Advent, Christmas, Lent, and Easter. They can also be used as part of family sessions that bring parents and middle graders together. They are best used in their entirety, though teachers may on occasion only have time for the scripture readings or only the guided meditation.

How To Prepare

You'll notice that each service has four readings, and part of each is from scripture. It's very important to practice with the four readers ahead of time so they can do justice to the readings. The suggested props for each service work to get the attention of the children as they enter the room, so you will want to have your prayer table set up before they enter. The suggested visuals help to develop the theme of the lesson.

If the children in your class are not familiar with guided meditation as a form of prayer, you may want to spend time before the prayer service practicing closing eyes, breathing, and being quiet. Don't attempt to lead them in prayer until they are quiet and calm.

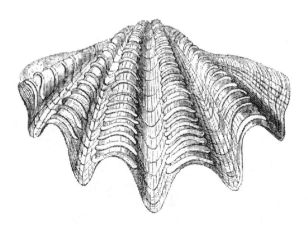

As you lead the meditation, be sure to speak clearly and dramatically, so that children can hear you and follow your directions. Also be sure to pause at the appropriate places (wherever there is an ellipsis), and try to sense when children have had enough time for one phase of the meditation before moving on to another. Invite children to bring to class a prayer journal (a notebook) so they can record their reactions to the meditation experience. Many find it easier to record their thoughts than to discuss them.

I hope that these services will help you and your classes to communicate with God more frequently. That is both my hope and my reward.

In closing, let me say that I drew heavily on scripture for these services, but also on other resources like the *Spiritual Exercises* of St. Ignatius and the wisdom of Thomas Aquinas and other great Christian minds. To these I am most grateful.

1
God's Gift of Joy

Materials Needed

For this service you will need copies of the introductory scripture reading for four readers. On your class prayer table place a Bible, a candle, a bowl of grapes or popcorn (or any small snack that might give children joy), and a picture or statue of an angel.

Leader　　　　God's gift of joy is an emotion of great delight. It is a feeling of happiness caused by something good or satisfying. Joy shows itself in the way we look, act, and speak. Scripture tells us God wants us to be joyful.

Reader One　　In the Old Testament we read that in spite of their trials in the desert, Moses instructed the Israelites to rejoice.

> *For seven days celebrate the Feast to the Lord your God at the place the Lord will choose. For the Lord your God will bless you in all your harvest and in all the work of your hands, and your joy will be complete (Deut 16:15).*

Reader Two　　When Jesus was born, an angel told the shepherds that great joy had come into the world.

> *The angel said to them, "Do not be afraid. I bring you good news of great joy that will be for all the people. Today in the town of David a savior has been born to you; he is Christ the Lord" (Lk 2:10–11).*

Reader Three Whenever a person is guided by the Holy Spirit, a special happiness is the result.

> *But the fruit of the Spirit is love, joy, peace, patience, kindness, goodness, faithfulness (Gal 5:22).*

Reader Four God wants us to be happy. One way to do this is—as the Bible says— is to keep our minds on good things.

> *Whatever is true, whatever is noble, whatever is right, whatever is pure, whatever is lovely, whatever is admirable—if anything is excellent or praiseworthy—think about such things (Phil 4:8).*

Leader There are many, many things in our lives that give us joy. Consider these grapes, for example (holding them up). I invite you to come forward and sample a grape from the prayer table as a reminder of all the wonderful gifts God gives for our pleasure.

Guided Meditation

Take a moment to get into a comfortable position. Close your eyes... Take three comfortable breaths and feel your body relaxing...

•Picture yourself as a happy child doing something you enjoyed. Were you jumping rope, riding a bike, playing a sport, or maybe just visiting with friends?...

•Part of who you are today is because of the joyful things of the past. Think about one special talent you have now that gives you and others joy...

•Consider the many beautiful gifts of nature you enjoy—like flowers... Do you ever give a flower to someone you like?...

• What foods give you joy? Pizza?... Ice cream?... Strawberries or bananas?...

• What music makes you feel joyous?... What other sounds bring you joy?...

• Take another deep breath... Relax... Carry your joy with you as we move to the future... Imagine that you are in the future, working at a job you enjoy... What job might that be?... Still in the future, still feeling that special inner joy, see yourself getting an award for a job well done... Imagine your employer and your coworkers praising your work...

• Now talk about your award with Jesus... What do you think he might say?... Perhaps he will invite you to celebrate at a special banquet with music, dancing, and good food... Best of all, feel the joy of being loved by Jesus... Take a few minutes to picture all of this in your mind... Are you filled with joy?...

• You will soon return to the everyday world. Hold this inner glow of joy as long as you can... Resolve from this day forward to try to find joy in places you didn't know it existed... Open your eyes now, back in this room.

Invite children to briefly share one of their particularly joyful moments. They may also want to record this in their prayer journals.

Closing Prayer

Light the candle on the prayer table and invite one of the children to hold the Bible as a sign that God gives us the gifts of joy.

Left Side   You, God, are the joy of the world. In your generosity and love you surprise us with reasons to celebrate and rejoice.

Right Side   You surround us with fresh air and trees, sunshine, flowers, and kind voices. You give us people who point the way to you, where we can find joy in your presence.

All   Even when we are sad, you promise to restore us. Thank you for making joy part of our heritage. Amen.

2
God's Gift
of Love

Materials Needed

For this service you will need copies of the introductory scripture readings for four readers. On your class prayer table place a candle and the Bible. Also place there small cutout hearts, one for each child.

Leader   God gives us the gift of love. Love is an emotion, a warm personal attachment, a feeling of affection for another. When we love someone, we want only good for that person. God is the greatest lover of all, and we share God's love all through our lives.

Reader One   God the Father showed how much he loved his son, Jesus, when he spoke from a cloud so all could hear.

> *While he was still speaking, a bright cloud enveloped them, and a voice from the cloud said, "This is my Son, whom I love; with him I am well pleased. Listen to him!" (Mt 17:5).*

Reader Two   Jesus spoke often of love. He said:

> *"Love the Lord your God with all your heart and with all your soul and with all your mind." This is the first and greatest commandment. And the second is like it: Love your neighbor as yourself (Mt 22:37–39).*

Reader Three   St. Paul describes how true lovers act:

> *Love is patient, love is kind. It does not envy,
> it does not boast, it is not proud. It is not rude,
> it is not self-seeking, it is not easily angered, it
> keeps no record of wrongs. Love does not
> delight in evil but rejoices with the truth... (1
> Cor 13:4–6).*

Reader Four   God promises us greater love someday than we could ever imagine. It is written:

> *No eye has seen, no ear has heard, no mind
> has conceived what God has prepared for
> those who love him (1 Cor 2:9).*

Invite children now to share a word or two about how someone's love has meant a great deal to them.

Guided Meditation

Get in a comfortable position... Close your eyes... Take three deep comfortable breaths and feel yourself relaxing...

•Picture yourself reclining on a comfortable couch... As you lie there, recall someone who loved you very much in the past. What did the person do?... How did you respond?...

•Consider some of the ways that Jesus helped others... Remember how he cured the sick? Remember the ten lepers?

•Now see Jesus standing in a boat as a storm rages... His disciples cry out for help... Jesus quiets the storm and commands the wind to die down... Was this an act of love?...

•Now see Jesus at a wedding party... He changes water to wine so the guests will have enough to drink... Was this an act of love?...

•Now see Jesus touching the eyes of a blind man... The man can see and is

8

rejoicing… Was this an act of love?…

•Now see Jesus bending down, writing in the sand, as he tells the people who want to throw stones at a sinful woman: "Let the one without sin throw the first stone"… Was this an act of love?…

•Now see Jesus hanging on the cross, getting ready to die… Jesus who did no wrong is being punished because he wanted to show us the way to God… What greater love can there be than this?

•Take a few moments now to talk to Jesus about all these gifts of love that he gave to others… and all the love he has given you…

•Ponder this great love for a while… And then when you are ready, return to the group…

Invite the children to discuss this experience if they seem interested in doing so. Or allow them to write about it in their prayer journals. Before reciting the Closing Prayer, have children come forward to receive one of the hearts. To each say, "Let this be a sign of Jesus' love for you."

Closing Prayer

Light the candle on the prayer table and invite the children to hold their small hearts as they pray—as a sign of just how much Jesus loves them.

Left Side   Dear gentle, loving Jesus, you showed us the way to live. You showed us by your actions how to love others.

Right Side   Love is a great gift from God. Love makes everything better in our lives. Help us to be unselfish with our love.

All   Keep us always ready to respond to your love. Amen.

3
God's Gift of Wisdom

Materials Needed

For this service you will need copies of the introductory scripture readings for four readers. On your class prayer table place the Bible and other books or symbols of wisdom (a dove, a story, a picture, a statue, etc.), and a candle.

Leader   God gives us the gift of wisdom, which helps us to make good decisions and to use all of our gifts and talents to the best of our ability.

Reader One   The wisdom sayings in the Bible help us to make wise decisions. Here are three of them:

> *Those who trust in God shall understand truth, and they shall abide with God in love (Wis 3:9).*
> *When we receive God's words and treasure God's commands, we shall be wise indeed (Prov 2:1–7).*
> *Do not gather up treasures for yourselves here on earth, rather seek the things of God (Mt 6:19–20).*

Reader Two   Jesus' stories are full of love and wisdom. In the story of the Prodigal Son he tells us how much God loves and welcomes us.

> *When the father saw his son coming—still a long way off—he ran to meet him. He embraced him and kissed him (Lk 15:20).*

Reader Three   Jesus is wisdom itself and he described himself in these words:

> *I am the way and the truth and the life. No one comes to the Father except through me (Jn 14:6).*

Reader Four   Sometimes Jesus spoke directly about what was wise.

> *Whoever can be trusted with very little can also be trusted with much, and whoever is dishonest with very little will also be dishonest with much (Lk 16:10).*

Invite children now to come forward to the prayer table and see if they can identify what the symbols placed there mean. Allow sufficient time for this.

Guided Meditation

Take a moment to get into a comfortable position... Close your eyes... Take three deep breaths and feel yourself relaxing...

•In your mind's eye imagine that you see a wide, deep, clear body of moving water and in the distance a large wooden raft moving in your direction... When the raft gets close enough, get on it and hang on as it drifts away from shore...

•Imagine yourself lying down on the raft as you watch the clouds. You feel very peaceful.

•All at once you see Jesus appearing in front of you, from out of a cloud. His arms are outstretched... He takes your hand and you begin to float up and away as part of the cloud... How does this feel? What are you thinking?...

•The cloud carries you and Jesus to a large building... and together you and Jesus leave the cloud and enter the building. There are shimmering golden shelves of books lining the walls... Some people hold books and seem to be reading...

•You realize that this is a building that people come to for wisdom… Jesus smiles at you and says, "Seek and you will find… Knock and the door will be opened…" Picture yourself breathing in all the wisdom you can… (longer pause)

•Talk to Jesus now about things you need in your life, areas where his gift of wisdom could help you right now, at school, at home, with your friends… Take all the time you need for this (longer pause)…

•All too soon Jesus walks with you out the other side of the building, and a cloud drifts by and you enter it… It drifts down, down toward the raft on the moving water…

•Soon you feel your feet resting on the wooden raft, which is drifting to shore, the same place where you entered it… You know it is time to leave the raft of wisdom…

•Your feet are on shore… You watch the raft drift away… And you are back in this room once again.

Ask children to relate experiences of wisdom they might have had. Challenge them to create a proverb that would fit the situation. Also, if they want to share their reaction to this prayer experience, invite them to do so.

Closing Prayer

Light the candle on the prayer table and invite several children to hold up some of the objects on your prayer table as a sign of God's wisdom and presence.

Left Side   Dear Jesus, exalted Son of God, thank you for the gift of wisdom. Help us to always rely on your wisdom before we make decisions.

Right Side   Help us to be wise in our relationships with others, including our enemies.

All   We want to be closer to you, wise and loving savior. Bless us with the wisdom of your Holy Spirit. Amen.

4

God's Gift
of Trust

Materials Needed

For this service you will need copies of the introductory scripture readings
for four readers. On your class prayer table place a candle, the Bible, and a
picture of an infant in its mother's arms.

Leader   God gives us the gift of trust. To trust someone is to
                  believe in their strength, ability, and integrity. To believe
                  in God is to trust God.

Reader One   The Bible tells us that when God's people were in trouble
                  they believed that God would help them.

> *And when the Israelites saw the great power*
> *the Lord displayed against the Egyptians,*
> *the people feared the Lord and put their trust*
> *in him and in Moses his servant (Ex 14:31).*

Reader Two   The Bible also warns where *not* to put our trust.

> *Do not trust in cheaters or take pride in*
> *stolen goods; though your riches increase, do*
> *not set your heart on them (Ps 62:11).*

Reader Three Scripture assures us that we can have confidence and trust
                  in God because of what God has done in the past.

> *At the beginning, O Lord, you established the*
> *earth, and the heavens are the work of your*
> *hands. They will perish, but you remain…*
> *(Heb 1:10–11).*

Reader Four   Jesus spoke clearly about how to handle fear with trust.

*Do not let your hearts be troubled. Trust in
God; trust also in me (Jn 14:1).*

Leader   I invite you to come forward one by one to look closely at the picture on our prayer table of the baby in its mother's arms. This child totally trusts the mother who carries it, just as you had to trust your parents as infants.

Guided Meditation

Close your eyes... Take three deep comfortable breaths... Feel yourself relaxing...

•Begin to slowly count backwards from ten to zero... As you count down you may feel yourself getting smaller and younger... 10...9...8...7...6...5...4...3...2...1... Now you are very small and very young. In your mind you are the size and state you were in before you were born...

•Imagine yourself back in your mother's womb... It is time for you to prepare to be born... You are floating in warm comfortable water... You can breathe easily... You are weightless... The Spirit of God, the giver of all life, is with you in this womb... Can you sense God's presence?

• All your needs are provided here… Your tummy is satisfied… Your body is not hot or cold, just comfortable… You can stretch as far as you want to… Feel your tiny body stretching… You can hear… Thump, thump, the beating of your own heart… You can hear the beating of your mother's heart, too…

• Deep inside your tiny body you have a soul… This is the part of you that connects to God… Imagine that with each breath you take your soul feels happy… Your soul knows that the air you breath is God's air… Can you feel the presence of God as you breathe?…

• Think about how it feels to be totally cared for… Think about how it makes you feel to be safe and comfortable…

• Imagine now that you feel God's hand touching your tiny hand… You know that someday your body will grow too big for this safe womb, but wherever you go, the Spirit of God will be with you…

• Though you may at times forget about God, God will never forget about you… God will always be close enough to touch your hand… Talk to God about this for a few minutes now… How does it make you feel to be so loved?…

• Enjoy this feeling of trust for a while… When you are ready, open your eyes and return to the group…

Invite the children to discuss this experience if they seem interested in doing so. Or, allow them to write about it in their prayer journals.

Closing Prayer

Light the candle on the prayer table and invite one of the children to hold up the picture of the infant as a sign that we can place our trust in God.

Left Side	Kind and gentle Spirit of God, thank you for being so close to us and watching over us.
Right Side	Teach us how to trust you always, and please continue to be near us.
All	We hold our outstretched hands to you. You know our needs and we trust that you will grant them. Amen.

5

God's Gift of Friends

Materials Needed

You will need copies of the readings for four readers. On your class prayer table, place a candle, the Bible, and a large loaf of bread for sharing later.

Leader A friend is someone who knows you well and is fond of you, a confidant, an ally, a chum, someone who will help you in time of need. Jesus is the best friend anyone could have.

Reader One All of us are God's special friends and God calls us by name. We know this from Scripture.

> *Abraham believed God… and he was called God's friend. And the Lord said to Moses, "I will do the very thing you have asked, because I am pleased with you and I know you by name" (Ex 33:17).*

Reader Two It was Christ who brought friendship to its highest form. He said to his followers:

> *My command is this: Love one another as I have loved you. There is no greater love than to lay down your lives for your friends. You are my friends if you do what I command. I no longer call you servants…. Instead, I have called you friends, for everything that I learned from my Father I have made known to you (Jn 15:12–15).*

Reader Three   Friends listen to one another. They don't quarrel, but they often discuss and disagree. Sometimes they compromise. Sometimes they let the one who seems best qualified decide.

> *Even though we speak like this, dear friends, we are confident of better things in your case—things that accompany salvation (Heb 6:9).*

Reader Four   Scripture discusses many incidents of friendship: writing letters, teaching, giving advice, having parties, being companions on a journey, caring for a sick friend, feeding each other, listening, even nagging can be the work of a friend.

Invite children to share examples of times when someone has been a true friend. In what ways have they been true friends to others?

Guided Meditation

Close your eyes…Take three deep comfortable breaths…Feel yourself relaxing…

•Imagine that you are in a large grassy field surrounded by beautiful shade trees…Sit down under one of these trees and feel the cool grass…

•As you sit there imagine that the field is filling up with people…they are greeting one another as friends. You see many of your own friends in the crowd…Thank God for them now…Picture yourself greeting your friends, enjoying their company…

•In the midst of the crowd, you can hear someone calling your name… "Friend," Jesus says, "Come and join me. Let's talk for a while."…

•Picture Jesus with his arms outstretched to you…See his smile…Hear the happiness in his voice as he calls you by name…

•You understand in this moment that Jesus loves you very much…He wants to be your best friend, to share your life, your joys, your sorrows, your problems…

•Think for a minute about one of the times that you may have experienced Jesus as a friend…and spend time now talking to him. Tell him whatever you want about your life right now, your friends, your concerns…

•When you are ready, picture yourself leaving the field, open your eyes, and return to the group.

Invite the children to discuss this experience if they seem interested in doing so. Or allow them to write about it in their prayer journals.

Closing Prayer

Light the candle on the prayer table and have one of the children hold up the bread as a reminder that Jesus, the Bread of Life, is our best friend.

Left Side Dear Jesus, having you as a friend gives us comfort and happiness. We don't like being alone. We want to share our lives with someone we can trust.

Right Side We want someone who will be there for us when we are in trouble, and we know you are that kind of friend for us.

All Thank you, kind and generous God, for all our friends, and thank you most of all for Jesus, our greatest friend. Amen.

Leader I invite you now to share this bread as a sign that Jesus is with us.

Break off or cut off pieces of the loaf and have the children distribute them to one another.

6

God's Gift of Healing

Materials Needed

For this service you will need copies of the introductory scripture readings for four readers. On your class prayer table place a candle, the Bible, and a small dish of oil as a symbol of the oils of healing used in church rituals.

Leader   God offers us the gift of healing for our minds, bodies, and spirits. Scripture tells us that God wants us to be well. We can do everything better when we feel well.

Reader One   Jesus came among us to destroy the powers of evil, so that we can be spiritually well. St. Paul wrote:

> Let us be self-controlled, putting on faith and love as a breastplate, and the hope of salvation as a helmet. For God did not appoint us to suffer wrath but to receive salvation through our Lord Jesus Christ (1 Thes 5:8–9).

Reader Two   Jesus did not neglect physical healing either. At least forty times scripture relates his compassion toward the physically sick.

> Jesus went throughout Galilee, teaching in their synagogues, preaching the good news of the kingdom, and healing every disease and sickness among the people (Mt 4:23).

Reader Three   Jesus offered love, compassion, and healing to many people. Scripture tells of a woman Jesus did not know who sneaked from behind to touch him.

> *"Who touched me?" Jesus asked. When they all denied it, Peter said, "Master, the people are crowding and pressing against you." But Jesus said, "Someone touched me; I felt power go out from me."*
>
> *Then the woman, seeing that she could not go unnoticed, came trembling and fell at his feet. In the presence of all the people, she told why she had touched him and how she had been instantly healed (Lk 8:45–48).*

Reader Four   As Jesus' followers, we are asked to heal others as he did. Here's what he said to his disciples:

> *Heal the sick, raise the dead, cleanse those who have leprosy, drive out demons. Freely you have received, so freely give (Mt 10:8).*

Invite children now to come to the prayer table and rub a little of the healing oil on their wrists. Encourage them to raise their hands to God in appreciation of good health. When all are back in their seats, begin the Guided Meditation.

Guided Meditation

Close your eyes… Take three deep, comfortable breaths and feel your body loosening, feeling freer… Do this three times.

•Imagine that you see Jesus on a road leading away from a town. A crowd of people is following him at a distance, but it's quiet except for the birds singing and a gentle breeze rustling the tall trees. Can you hear them?

•Imagine now that Jesus turns to the crowd and motions for them to follow… You begin to follow, too, and you blend in with the moving crowd… You notice that some in the crowd are in dirty and ragged clothes… Some in the group are wearing boots… Some are barefoot…

•Cross-legged, sitting on the side of the road is a young man watching the crowd. He is deaf and he cannot speak. Watch a few seconds as he tries to signal Jesus with his hands.

•Jesus sees the man and he walks to where he is sitting. "What do you need?" he asks the man… The man points to his ears and mouth.

•Jesus touches his ears and his tongue and the man can hear and speak. Joyfully the cured man falls in behind Jesus…

•Imagine that also in the crowd is a young woman whose feet are swollen and bleeding. Jesus goes over to her and looks at her feet. He kneels next to her and takes mud and water from the side of the road and packs her feet in the mixture. When he removes the mud pack, her feet are healed. The young woman is so happy, she, too, begins to follow Jesus.

•Now imagine that Jesus sees you there, watching him…He approaches you…He says, "What can I heal in your life?"…

Talk to Jesus about this. Say whatever comes to your mind… When you are ready, open your eyes and return to this room.

Invite the children to discuss what they learned about Jesus as he healed them. What did they learn about their own needs?

Closing Prayer

Light the candle on the prayer table and invite one of the children to hold up the oil as a sign of God's healing presence.

Left Side	Loving and giving Jesus, you are a great healer. Every day as we walk the path of life, we meet people who need healing. Please help us to reach out to them as you would have us do.
Right Side	Help us always to remember that you want us to be well and that all healing begins with you.
All	We believe that when we need healing and ask for it, you will give it to us. Amen.

7
God's Gift of the Heart

Materials Needed

On the class prayer table place a large picture of a human heart or a picture of the Sacred Heart of Jesus. Also place a Bible and a candle on the table. You will need copies of the readings for the four readers.

Leader　　　One of God's great gifts to us is a beating heart. The heart is the muscle that keeps blood flowing throughout our bodies. It gives us energy and good health. But the heart is also considered the seat of emotions and feelings.

Reader One　　The Bible teaches us that God looks at what is in our hearts.

The Lord does not look at the things we look at. We look at the outward appearance, but the Lord looks at the heart (1 Sam 16:7).

Reader Two　　Just as love is felt in the heart, so is fear and respect (or honor). The Bible teaches us to treat God with honor as we should treat everyone who nurtures us.

But be sure to serve God faithfully with all your heart; consider what great things God has done for you (1 Sam 12:24).

Reader Three	No matter how we plan or hope for something, it is still God who makes the final decision as to whether or not it will happen.

> *In our hearts we plan our course, but the Lord determines our steps (Prov 16:9).*

Reader Four	When trouble comes, the smart thing to do, as Jesus did, is to ask the Father for help.

> *Now my heart is troubled, and what shall I say? "Father, save me from this hour?" No, it was for this very reason I came to this hour. Not my will, but yours, be done (Jn 12:27).*

Leader	I ask you now to stand and put your hand over your heart. Feel it beating. After a moment take your hand away and rest it on your wrist. Can you still feel the beat of your heart?

Guided Meditation

Take a moment to get into a comfortable position…Relax and close your eyes…Take three deep comfortable breaths and feel yourself relaxing more and more…

•Again put your hand over your heart and feel it beating… Keep it there for a few seconds…

•Imagine what your heart looks like… See its rich red color… Can you hear its rhythmic sounds?…

•Each heart has a sound—like a song—that is all its own… Listen for the song of your heart… Can you hear it?…

•This beating heart is keeping you alive and full of energy… The song in your heart is what keeps you joyful…

•Recall now someone who loves you…. Your heart has a song for this person… Picture the face of this person… Spend a little time thinking about him or her…

•Though you are loved very much by the people around you, remember that you are also loved by Jesus. In a way, he has a piece of your heart. With your inner eyes examine your heart more carefully…

•The piece of your heart that belongs to Jesus is one that only he can fill…

Picture Jesus' radiant heart next to your heart… beating out of love for you… sending out waves of love to you…

•Listen now as Jesus speaks to you. He says: "Lift up your heart to me… You are mine: I will be with you always… As the Father has loved me, so do I love you."

•Take a few minutes now to think about Jesus and to respond to his love for you…

•When you are ready open your eyes and remove your hand from your heart…

Invite children to discuss this experience if they seem interested in doing so. Or allow them to write about it in their prayer journals. Before closing, recite the Closing Prayer together.

Closing Prayer

Light the candle on the prayer table and invite one of the children to hold up the picture of the Sacred Heart or the Bible as a sign of God's presence.

Left Side   Oh, precious heart of Jesus, thank you for listening and for understanding when our hearts hurt.

Right Side   Help us to remember to honor and respect those who love and nurture us.

All   Please keep your beating heart close to ours so together we may sing out in love and joy. Amen.

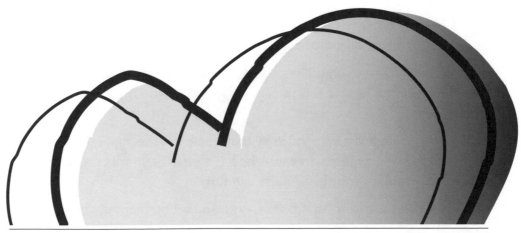

8
God's Gift of Water

Materials Needed

For this service you will need copies of the readings (for the four readers) and a container of water, which can be placed on your class prayer table. If possible, also place there a Bible and a candle.

Leader   Water is a precious gift from God. Without it we can't survive. We use it to quench our thirst and to water our plants. It nourishes and sustains every living creature on Earth.

Reader One The Bible teaches us that God created water before creating people.

> *Now the earth was formless and empty, darkness was over the surface of the deep, and the Spirit of God was hovering over the waters (Gen 1:2).*

Reader Two Jesus spoke of the Holy Spirit as water.

> *Whoever believes in me, as scripture has said, streams of living water will flow from within that person (Jn 7:38).*

Reader Three   God created all things, including the gift of water. The Bible teaches us that we will only have a good, rich, and full life if we welcome the "streams of living waters," that is, the Holy Spirit flowing within us.

Reader Four   Jesus used the symbol of water as he taught his apostles. He changed water to wine; he calmed the seas and he walked on water. He taught the woman at the well the importance of receiving God's living water.

Leader   I invite you to come forward now to touch the water in this container. Think about how it feels, how it looks, and what its uses might be.

After all have touched the water, invite children to comment on their reactions. Then continue as below.

Guided Meditation

Take a moment or two to get in a comfortable position. Relax and close your eyes... Take three deep comfortable breaths and feel yourself relaxing more and more....

•Imagine the feeling of warm water all around your body...

•Imagine yourself floating in a warm blue ocean... Hold this feeling as you smell the salt air blowing over you.

•Imagine that you can taste the salt water on your lips...and hear the sounds the ocean makes in your ears...

•Feel the water relaxing you until you can't tell the difference between you and the ocean...

•Remember that God created these waters, as God created all things...

•Think of yourself as a small but very important part of the sea. You are constantly changing in shape and movement, rolling with the waves. You are one with the sea... Stay with this good feeling for a little while...

•As you feel the power of the ocean water all around you, recall that the power of the Spirit of God is working in your life, all around you, always...

•Think about a time when you sensed God working with you or sensed God flowing around you. Stay with these thoughts as you continue to gently roll with the sea...

•How does the strength of the sea remind you of God's power?…of God's care for you? Do you feel closer to God as you trust the water to carry you forth?… Spend time talking to God now, saying anything that is on your mind… (longer pause here).

•Imagine that you are coming to the shore now, ending your time in the water… As soon as you are ready, you can open your eyes.

Invite children to discuss this experience if they seem interested in doing so. Or allow them to write about it in a prayer journal. Before closing, recite the Closing Prayer together.

Closing Prayer

Light the candle on the prayer table and invite one of the children to hold up the Bible as a sign of God's presence.

Left Side	Father, thank you for helping us to recognize your power, which is even more awesome than the sea. Thank you for your Word that reveals this power to us.
Right Side	Surround us with your strength, your care, and your Holy Spirit. Watch over us and help us to use the gift of water, which you so generously provide, with great care.
All	Thank you for the great gift of water. Amen.

9

God's Gift of the Cross

Materials Needed

For this service you will need four copies of the introductory scripture readings. On your class prayer table place a Bible, a large cross, a candle, and a basket in which the children can place their "troubles," which they will write out during this service.

Leader   For us Christians, the cross is the symbol of Christ's death by crucifixion. It is a sign of Christ's love for us. It also reminds us that every person's life is made up of joy as well as suffering, and that Jesus shares our crosses and lightens our load.

Reader One   Jesus' command to take up the cross and follow him is a spiritual lesson for all of us. He said:

> *Those who do not take up their crosses and follow me are not worthy of me. Those who find their life will lose it, and those who lose their life for my sake will find it (Mt 10:38–39).*

Reader Two   Many of us would like a God who only makes us feel good, but the Bible teaches that this is not possible. As Paul once said,

> *I have often told you before… that many live as enemies of the cross of Christ… Their minds are on earthly things. But our citizenship is in heaven. And we eagerly await a*

Savior from there, the Lord Jesus Christ…
(Phil 3:18–4:1).

Reader Three   At some point in our lives we all will experience difficulties. At times like these we are asked to hang on and trust, as Jesus did from the cross.

> *About the ninth hour Jesus cried out in a loud voice…: "My God, my God, why have you forsaken me?" (Mt 27:46).*

Reader Four   As he hung upon the cross, Jesus realized that most of his friends had run away in fear. He looked, as well, at the ones who tortured him. To all of them he said,

> *Father, forgive them, for they do not know what they are doing (Lk 23:34).*

Now invite each child to write on a small slip of paper one thing that he or she finds difficult right now, in a word, one of their "troubles." (They need not sign these slips.) Ask them to place the slips in the basket on your prayer table.

Guided Meditation

Close your eyes… Take a deep breath… Try to relax your body and mind…

•Recall the "trouble" that you wrote on the slip of paper. Imagine this difficulty taking the shape of a cross that you will carry on your shoulder. Feel its weight as you picture yourself walking along…

•Nearby there is a road that leads to a hill… A crowd of people are gathering there… Still carrying your cross, walk over and join the crowd, which seems to be an angry crowd… They are cursing and spitting at a man wearing a crown of thorns… This man carries a large heavy wooden cross…

•Take a good look at this man… You recognize him; you know in your heart that this is Jesus… How does it feel to see him like this?…

•Suddenly Jesus turns toward you… His eyes look directly into yours… A blaze of light shines from his eyes as though he is speaking to you through the light. "Will you help me carry my cross?" he seems to be asking…

•Suddenly you surge forward past the soldiers and reach for the cross to pull it off his back, but your own cross slows you down… Before you can help Jesus the soldiers grab you and push you back… But you see Jesus meeting your eye again… The light shines through…

•You want so much to help Jesus, but you know it's not possible now… You watch as he is pushed forward toward Calvary, but you can still feel the light of his presence… His eyes meet yours again…

•What do you think Jesus is telling or asking you?… What thoughts and feelings are coming through?… Ponder this for a while…(longer pause)

•When you are ready open your eyes and return to the group…

Closing Prayer

Light the candle. Invite one of the children to hold up the cross from the prayer table. Another one or two could hold up the container filled with the written troubles.

Left Side   Dear savior, Jesus, it is so hard to carry our troubles on our backs, and so we offer them to you. Help us to carry them with courage and patience.

Right Side   You are the Son of God, and you know that by our behavior we are sometimes crosses for others to bear. Forgive us when we fail in this way.

All   Please help us to understand your love, and to imitate you by sharing our love with everyone we meet. Please help us with all our difficulties. Amen.

10
God's Gift
of the Law

Materials Needed

For this service you will need copies of the four introductory scripture readings. On a large poster print the Ten Commandments and the New Commandment from Jesus (see text below). Display this prominently on your class prayer table. Also place there a Bible and a candle.

Leader   God's gift of the Ten Commandments is only part of the spiritual laws we have received. Laws protect us and guide us in our relationships with God and others.

Reader One   God gave the Ten Commandments first to Moses and then to all the people. Scripture says:

> *The Lord wrote on these tablets what was written before, the Ten Commandments that were proclaimed to you on the mountain...*
> *(Deut 10:4).*

Reader Two   This is what Jesus said about the law when a teacher asked which was the most important commandment.

> *The most important one is this: "Hear, O Israel, the Lord our God is one. Love the Lord your God with all your heart and with all your soul and with all your mind and with all your strength" (Mk 12:28–31).*

Reader Three   Jesus had great respect for the law and he always submitted himself to the will of the Heavenly Father. Scripture says:

When the time had fully come, God sent his Son, born of a woman, born under the law, to redeem those under the law, that we might receive the full rights of God's children (Gal 4:4–5).

Reader Four As we grow older and wiser, we realize that laws protect us from trouble. They help us to form right relationships, especially the new law given by Jesus at the Last Supper. He said:

Love one another as I have loved you (Jn 15:12).

Now invite children to slowly walk one at a time up to the prayer table to review the Ten Commandments and the new commandment from Jesus. When all have reviewed these laws, share the following meditation.

Guided Meditation

Close your eyes… Take a few deep breaths and feel yourself relaxing… Feel your shoulders becoming lighter… Feel your fingers loosen…

•Imagine yourself starting up a mountain path… Picture yourself taking ten steps and then ten more, stepping… one… two… three… four… five… six… seven… eight… nine… ten…

•Now rest and look around at the mountain, at the bushes and shrubbery surrounding the trail… Enjoy the scenery a minute before you continue the climb… As you once again climb the path, take ten more steps before you stop to rest…

•Imagine that far in the distance you see a bush that is on fire… Notice that the fire is not hurting the bush… It's coming up through the bush somehow. Recall that it was from a burning bush that God first spoke to Moses.

•Move closer to the burning bush and imagine that you hear the voice of God. God is inviting you to reflect on the Ten Commandments and the new commandment of Jesus

•Recall one of these commandments and think about what it means to you... How has it affected your life?...

•Seat yourself comfortably near the burning bush and talk to God about how laws affect you, at home, at school, and elsewhere...

•Also talk to God about the new commandment that Jesus gave: "Love one another as I have loved you." Spend as much time as you need on this...

•When you are finished find the trail again and go back down the mountain... Open your eyes and return to the group.

Invite children to discuss their experience if they choose. Have they ever had to pay the consequences for breaking one of God's laws? Or suggest that they write about this experience in their prayer journals.

Closing Prayer

Light the candle on the prayer table and invite one of the children to hold up the Commandments as a sign of respect for God and God's law.

Left Side   Dear God the Father, thank you for the Ten Commandments and for all the laws you give us because you love us.

Right Side   We thank you for Jesus and for his message of love. Help us to learn how to love one another as Jesus loves us.

All   Please help us to listen to you always—whether you speak to us from a burning bush, our parents, teachers, or one another. Amen.

11

God's Gift of Light

Materials Needed

For this service you will need copies of the introductory readings for the four readers. On your class prayer table place a candle, a Bible, and a flashlight.

Leader	God's gift of light makes things visible. All the colorful things we can see depend on light. God made the light for us to enjoy the beauty of flowers, mountains, streams, and rainbows. God also gave us the light of faith, so that we might place our trust in God throughout our lives.
Reader One	Scripture tells us: *God saw that the light was good, and God separated the light from the darkness (Gen 1:4).*
Reader Two	For Christians, light is the symbol of truth, faith, wisdom, virtue, grace, charity, and all other spiritual qualities that signify the presence of Christ. St. John wrote: *Whoever lives by the truth comes into the light, so that it may be seen plainly that what Jesus has done has been done through God (Jn 3:21).*
Reader Three	Anyone who does God's work is a light to the world. Matthew's gospel says:

People don't light a lamp and put it under a bowl. Rather they put it on its stand, and it gives light to everyone in the house. In the same way, let your light shine before others, that they may see your good deeds and praise your Father in heaven (Mt 5:15–16).

Reader Four   Light conveys to the human mind a sense of joy, optimism, goodness, purity, beauty, festiveness, dignity, and life. In one of his letters, St. Paul said:

The works you do will be visible to all, for the light of day will reveal them (Rom 13:12–14).

Leader   At this time we will turn off all the lights in the room, except the candle on the prayer table and the flashlight. Be conscious of the differences in color and shading because of the light made by both.

If possible, leave the lights off for the guided meditation.

Guided Meditation

Close your eyes… Take a deep breath and feel yourself relaxing… The word light also means of little weight, not heavy, a light load… Try to feel this way about your body; feel it lighten…

•See a golden light hovering above your head… See the light glowing, pulsating, as it hovers above the crown of your head…

•Imagine that this light is the light of God… See it beginning to expand, to grow larger and to mix with the atoms in motion within and surrounding your head… See this halo of light settling down on the top of your head… Feel your own spirit merging, becoming one with it…

•Feel the sense of peace this light brings… It is a joyous feeling, like when something wonderful has just happened to you… Take another deep breath… Your face should now be completely relaxed… You are now going into a deeper and healthier level of mind…

•Imagine now that this golden light is spreading downward from your head into your face and neck… Feel the comforting heat coming from it… Feel the light spreading throughout your entire body and let it remind you that God is very near…

•Let a sense of lightness and joy take over your body… This joy is the feeling you get when God is merged in your light… God knows you better than anyone… God knows you better than you know yourself…

•God always sees the best in you, the finest you… You know you have this side of you, but you cannot always see it…

•Spend a few minutes talking with God now. Thank God for the gift of Light and tell God whatever you want…

•When you are finished open your eyes and return to the group…

Invite the children to discuss this experience if they seem interested in doing so. Or allow them to write about it in their prayer journals.

Closing Prayer

Leave the candle burning brightly on your prayer table, and invite one of the children to hold up the flashlight as a sign of God's gift of light.

Left Side	Dear God, you brighten the whole world because you are the giver of life and light.
Right Side	We need you to shine on our lives so we can understand more, do better, and stay in the warmth of your love.
All	Thank you for your light and for all your gifts to us. Amen.

12

God's Gift of Counsel

Materials Needed

For this service you will need copies of the introductory scripture readings for four readers. On your prayer table place the Bible, a candle, and, if available, a picture of Jesus. Also have there a small box or container in which children may later place slips of paper.

Leader	Scripture teaches us that Jesus is the greatest counselor or guide that ever lived. When we are troubled or confused God wants us to be able to receive help. A good counselor is someone we can trust, and we can trust Jesus more than anyone.
Reader One	Many of the prophets were good counselors. When King David broke God's law, the prophet Nathan was sent by God to correct David's behavior. Nathan scolded David:
	Why did you despise the Word of the Lord by doing what is evil in God's eyes (2 Sam 12:9)?
Reader Two	The prophet Isaiah foretold of the coming of the greatest counselor of all:
	For to us a child is born, to us a son is given…

and he will be called Wonderful, Counselor,
Mighty God, Everlasting Father, Prince of
Peace (Is 9:5).

Reader Three   Jesus knew how to handle very difficult situations, like when a woman who was caught in sin was about to be stoned. He turned to her accusers and counseled them: *"If any one of you is without sin, you can be the first to throw a stone at her" (Jn 8:7).* And no one threw a stone.

Reader Four   Before Jesus was crucified he promised his followers that they would not be left without help and counsel.

The Counselor, the Holy Spirit, whom the
Father will send in my name, will teach you
all things and will remind you of everything
I have said to you (Jn 14:26).

Leader   I invite you now to think about a person you trust, someone you can talk to and get advice from. What quality do you like most about this person? Write it on a slip of paper and then drop it in the container on our prayer table.

Guided Meditation

Take three deep comfortable breaths and feel yourself relaxing... You are going to a deeper healthier level of mind, a more spiritual place where you will meet your counselor...

•Imagine yourself walking toward a closed door... Behind that door is your private counseling room...; open the door and go into the room... Picture the walls, the floor, the furniture. How do they look?

•Find a comfortable place to sit in this private room... Relax... Take another deep breath... Remember that this is your private place where no one can disturb you...

•Listen now for a knock on the door... It is Jesus, your counselor. If you want him to enter your room now, open the door and invite him into the room... Ask him to sit down with you...

•Remember that Jesus is the Great Counselor... Is there something you want to discuss with him? Have you done something you feel bad or confused about, that you want to share with him? Feel free to tell him about whatever is on your mind... (longer pause)

•Now spend time listening to Jesus. What do you think he wants to say to you?...

•When you have finished your discussion with Jesus, thank him for being your counsclor... Say good-bye to him for now, remembering you can invite him into your room whenever you choose...

•When you are ready, leave your private room and return to this class.

Invite children to discuss this experience if they wish or to record their thoughts in their prayer journals.

Closing Prayer
Light the candle on the prayer table and invite one of the children to hold up the Bible as a sign that God is always willing to counsel us.

Left Side   Wonderful Counselor, Mighty God, we thank you for all the information and advice you have given us so far in our lives.

Right Side   Knowing we can trust you with anything helps us to be more open about our problems and to look to the example of Jesus for solutions.

All   Thank you for giving us Jesus, your son, to guide and counsel us. Amen.

13
God's Gift of Perseverance

Materials Needed

For this service you will need copies of the introductory scripture readings for the four readers. On the class prayer table you will need a Bible, a candle, water, and an apple. If possible, also have a dish of apple seeds.

Leader   God gives us the gift of perseverance, which means "hanging in there." It combines physical strength with the courage to hang on to God's way, no matter what.

Reader One   Scripture tells us about people who persevered. Remember the three wise men? They would not go home until they had followed the star that led to the promised savior.

Reader Two   Jesus told this story of a woman who persevered:

In a certain town there was a judge who neither feared God nor anyone else. And there was a widow in that town who kept coming to him with the plea, "Grant me justice against my adversary." For some time he refused. But finally he said to himself, "Even though I don't fear God or care about people, yet because this widow keeps bothering me, I will see that she gets justice, so that she won't eventually wear me out with her coming" (Lk 18:1–5).

Reader Three   The Bible also relates many incidents of healing that came about because people prayed and did not give up.

As Jesus approached Jericho, a blind man was sitting by the roadside begging. When he heard the crowd going by, he asked what was happening. They told him, "Jesus of Nazareth is passing by." He called out, "Jesus, Son of David, have mercy on me!" Those who led the way rebuked him and told him to be quiet, but he shouted all the more, "Son of David, have mercy on me!"

Jesus stopped and ordered the man to be brought to him. When he came near, Jesus asked him, "What do you want me to do for you?" "Lord, I want to see," he replied. Jesus said to him, "Receive your sight; your faith has healed you" (Lk 18:35–42).

Reader Four Jesus encourages us, too, to keep believing that God hears us and cares about us:

Ask and it will be given to you; seek and you will find; knock and the door will be opened to you. For everyone who asks receives; those who seek find; and to those who knock, the door will be opened (Mt 7:7–8).

Leader (Hold up the apple from your prayer table.)
I'll bet you never thought about it, but unless a piece of fruit like this apple hangs in there, it does not ripen. I invite you come up and touch the seeds and the apple on our prayer table. Note the apple's shape and its skin. Think how long it took to grow this beautiful piece of fruit.

Guided Meditation

Take a moment to get into a comfortable position… Relax and let go of your worries… Close your eyes… Take three deep comfortable breaths…

•Imagine yourself holding an apple seed, like the ones on our prayer table, and look for a piece of ground where you can plant it, a place where the seed will not be disturbed so it can grow in peace and quiet, protected by God's gift of sun and rain…

•Plant your seed now… deep enough so it is secure, yet shallow enough so the rain and sun will reach the ground that will nourish it…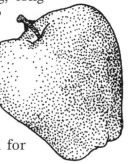

•The roots of your seed need to reach deep into the ground. They require darkness… The action of the seed is hidden at this time, but imagine how it must be growing. See it sprouting and picture yourself visiting it often, watching and watering for a long, long time. How does this waiting feel? Why do you have to wait so long for this tree to grow?

•You see that growth is happening because day by day, week by week, your apple tree is getting larger… You have loved and cared for this tree because you planted it.

•Now see the tree at full size… Picture the apples on its branches, how delicious they look.

•See yourself picking one of them, taking a bite. Note the taste and the crunch. When you bite close to the center, see the seeds there.

•This fruit you are eating is your reward for the love and care you gave the seed and the small tree… Because you persevered, you can see the results of your labor. Talk to God now in your own words about this gift of fruit… Ask God to help you to "hang in there" for all the important tasks of your life… (longer pause)

•Open your eyes and know that you are back in this room.

Invite children to share this experience if they wish or to write about it in their prayer journals.

Closing Prayer

Light the candle on the prayer table and invite one of the children to hold up the apple and another to hold up the container of seeds—as signs that all good things are worth waiting for.

Left Side   Thank you, loving God, for all your gifts, especially for the gift of perseverance. Remind us often that we are supposed to keep trying, to persevere in all the life tasks you have given us.

Right Side   Jesus, you are our model. You never gave up. Please give us the strength to keep going as we journey through life.

All   Thank you, God, for the gift of fruit that takes so long to grow. Thank you for all your gifts. Amen.

14
God's Gift
of Hands

Materials Needed

For this service you will need copies of the introductory scripture readings for four readers. On your class prayer table place a candle, the Bible, and a picture or statue of praying hands.

Leader   God has given us the wonderful gift of hands. With our hands we are able to grasp, grip, seize, or hold any object we care about. We can write with our hands, turn pages to read, and touch someone we love. Each of us has hands that are unique and special.

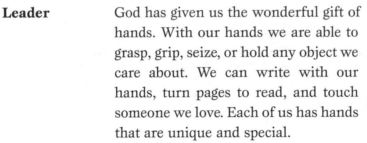

Reader One   God breathed on us to give us life, but God did even more. Scripture says:

> *See, I have engraved you on the palms of my hands; you are ever before me (Is 49:16).*

Reader Two   At some time in our life we may feel that no one cares about us, but God will always care for us. This is God's promise:

> *I give them eternal life, and they shall never perish; no one can snatch them out of my hand (Jn 10:28).*

Reader Three   Just as we hold out our hands to help people we care about, Scripture tells of many instances when Jesus held out his hand to those he loved. Recall that Peter tried to walk across the water to Jesus.

> *But when he saw the wind, he was afraid and, beginning to sink, cried out, "Lord, save me!" Immediately Jesus reached out his hand and caught him. "You of little faith," he said, "why did you doubt?" (Mt 14:30–31)*

Reader Four   Scripture tells us that God made us but God is more than our creator.

> *O Lord, you are our Father. We are the clay, you are the potter; we are the work of your hands (Is 64:7).*

Leader: I invite you now to hold up your hands. Flex them and feel the power in them. Think for a minute about what your hands have helped you do this very day. What one particular thing impressed you most? (pause) Now gently clap the shoulder of the person on your right as a reminder that your hands can also give comfort and joy to others.

Guided Meditation

Close your eyes... Take three deep breaths... Feel yourself relaxing, letting go of any fears or concerns you may have...

•Now picture a white glow above your head... See this glow expanding and changing shape, forming two large, strong glowing hands... Imagine that these hands are the hands of God...

•Watch these hands as they move, gathering a mound of earth, shaping and forming this mound... Watch as these strong glowing hands shape the mound of earth into a figure that looks like you...

•See how lovingly those hands work… See how gentle, but firm they are… See the figure of yourself emerging from those hands… and look at what a wonderful creation you are…

•See your feet… See them move… Look at your hands… Notice their shape, color, and size…

•Are your hands anything like those large, strong, glowing hands of God?… Think about all the things your hands can do… Think about all the objects your hands can hold… Think about what you wish your hands could do…

•Notice again the strong, glowing hands above you… God is there as promised… Reach up your hands to God's hands… See God's hands moving closer to yours…

•In your imagination, touch God's large, strong, glowing hands and hold on to them. Can you find your name engraved on the palms of God's hands?…

•Rest in God's hands a while, feeling protected by their gentle touch… Talk to God in your own words for a few minutes… (longer pause)

•Remember you can always return to those strong, protective hands of God any time you want to pray…

•Open your eyes now, back in this room.

Invite children to share this experience if they wish or to record it in their prayer journals.

Closing Prayer

Light the candle on the prayer table. Ask one of the children to hold the Bible as a sign of God's presence. Invite children to raise their hands, palms up as they repeat this prayer after you.

Leader   Dearest helpful God, whose hands always reach out to us, we thank you for your love. We thank you for the gift of our hands, which can do so many things. Help us to always use them well, in a way that will please you. Amen.

15
God's Gift of Covenant

Materials Needed

For this service you will need copies of the scripture readings for the four readers. On your class prayer table place the Bible, a candle, and symbols of God's covenant with us, for example: food, water, a plant, a picture of a sunny day, etc.

Leader   God's covenant with us is a serious and binding agreement. In it God promises to watch over us and care for us when we are faithful to God's law.

Reader One   In scripture we hear these words that God spoke to Abraham:

> *I will establish my covenant as an everlasting covenant between me and you and your descendants after you, for all generations to come, to be your God and the God of your descendants after you (Gen 17:6–7).*

Reader Two   God became so angry with the behavior of the people during Noah's day that the world was destroyed by a flood that filled the earth. Noah was a good man, however.

> *Noah did all that the LORD commanded him. And God protected him during the flood and placed a rainbow in the sky as a sign of the everlasting covenant between God and all living creatures of every kind on the earth (Gen 7:5, Gen 9:16).*

Reader Three   Scripture reminds us our covenant with God is a covenant of friendship that will last forever.

> *Those who confide in God are God's friends and God will make a lasting covenant with them (Ps 25:14).*

Reader Four   Jesus came among us as a sign of the New Covenant. From Jesus we understand more about God's love and promises.

> *In the same way, after the supper he took the cup, saying, "This cup is the new covenant in my blood, which is poured out for you" (Lk 22:20).*

Leader   I invite you now to come up to the prayer table to see and touch some of the gifts that are signs of God's everlasting covenant with us.

Guided Meditation

Take a moment to get into a comfortable position… Close your eyes… Take three deep breaths… Feel yourself relaxing…

•Imagine yourself in a room that is very comfortable, a private place where you won't be disturbed… Hear gentle music in the background…

•Listen now for footsteps… A knock… Jesus wants to share this special space with you, but he respects your privacy. He will never enter your private space without your invitation…

•Imagine that you hear his strong but gentle voice calling your name as he knocks at your door… Recall what Jesus said in scripture:

"Here I am! I stand at the door and knock. When those who hear my voice open the door, I will come in and eat with them…" (Rev 3:20).

•Do you want Jesus to be part of your everyday life, to guide you and help you with decisions?… Do you want a personal covenant with Jesus?…

•If your answer is "yes" answer his call… Open the door to a more special friendship with him….

•Picture Jesus in this room with you… Feel relaxed and comfortable as you would with a friend. Tell Jesus everything that is in your heart and mind.

Listen while Jesus talks to you about God's great love for you and God's promise to watch over you. . .

•Talk to Jesus now about what you hope for from God… Tell him what you care most about…and, again, listen for his answer…

•Spend as much time as you want talking with Jesus… Whatever you share at this time is for you alone to ponder in your heart…

•When you are ready, open your eyes, remembering Jesus and the New Covenant, as you come back to this room.

Invite children to discuss this experience if they choose. Or allow them to write about it in their prayer journals.

Closing Prayer

Light the candle on your prayer table and invite one of the children to hold up the Bible as a sign of God's presence and everlasting covenant.

Left Side   Dear Jesus, you are the Son of God, but you are also our friend. Teach us how to be loyal friends to you and help us to be faithful to God's covenant.

Right Side   You offer us a new covenant based on love, Jesus, come into our lives, and show us how to share your love with others.

All   Thank you, God, for your promises to us. Thank you especially for the gift of Jesus, your Son. Amen.

16
God's Gift of Darkness

Materials Needed

For this service you will need copies of the introductory scripture readings for four readers. On your class prayer table place the Bible, a candle, a map, a large flashlight.

Leader   God's gift of darkness allows us to see the stars, to sleep, and to appreciate the light of day. Both light and darkness are part of the cycle of life.

Reader One   The Bible teaches that even when there is great darkness God is present.

> *Now the earth was formless and empty, darkness was over the surface of the deep, and the Spirit of God was hovering over the waters (Gen 1:2).*

Reader Two   Scripture also teaches that even when it seemed that everything was lost in darkness God took care of the Israelites.

> *Total darkness covered all Egypt for three days. No one could see anyone else or go out for three days. Yet all the Israelites had light in the places where they lived (Ex 10:22–23).*

Reader Three   The image of darkness is sometimes associated with evil. But even in darkness, God knows the secrets of a person's heart.

> *Woe to those who go to great depths to hide their plans from the Lord, who do their work in darkness and think, "Who sees us? Who will know?" (Is 29:15).*

Reader Four   After the resurrection of Christ his followers were told:

> *You are a chosen people, a royal priesthood, a holy nation, a people belonging to God, that you may declare the praises of the one who called you out of darkness into wonderful light (1 Pt 2:9).*

At this time ask children to come forward to examine the map and the flashlight. Ask if they have ever used a map. Have they ever been lost and found their way because of a map? Has a flashlight ever led them safely somewhere in the dark?

Guided Meditation

Close your eyes... Take three deep comfortable breaths... Relax and feel your worries and fears drifting away...

•Imagine yourself standing outside a deep dark cave... Inside there is no light, so you will only be able to feel and hear to get around...

•Put your hands against an imaginary wall and begin to feel yourself entering the cave... Move deeper into the cave... The walls are rounded and a bit wet... The floor is smooth, except for an occasional stone...

•Imagine that the slope of the cave is deeper now... You are moving down at a little faster rate... What do you hear? What do you smell inside the cave?... Do you feel frustrated? Do you feel trapped?

•Keeping your eyes closed, imagine that your eyes are fully

open, but still all is darkness… What are your thoughts and feelings now?…
Even in this darkness, do you believe that God is with you?…

•Suddenly you find yourself at a part of the cave where there is a wall in front of you and beside you… You don't know which way to go… You feel around for an opening… Listen for echoes or sounds that might give you a clue to where you are… Smell, and use every sense you can to understand your surroundings and how you can move forward…

•Do not let fear of the darkness trap you into thinking you are stuck… Pause in the darkness and call on God… Be still and know that God is very near, even in the dark… Talk to God about how to find your way in this cave and in other circumstances of your life. Take all the time you need for this… (longer pause)

•Imagine now that God hands you a flashlight and a map and when you study the map you see that going forward would be circling your way back to the entrance of the cave… And so you go forward with God's help.

•Once you are out of the cave, open your eyes and return to the group.

Invite the children to discuss this experience. They might want to talk about the darkest place they have ever been. What was the worst thing about it? Did they remember that they were not alone, even in the darkest moment?

Closing Prayer

Light the candle on the class prayer table. Ask one child to hold up the map and another to hold up the flashlight as signs that God guides us on our journey.

Left Side   Dear heavenly Father, you always overcome darkness. Help us to remember that you are with us always—in light as well as darkness.

Right Side   Thank you for guiding us by your holy Word. Thank you, too, for candlelight, for flashlights, and for maps that give us direction.

All   Our world is sometimes full of gloom and ignorance. Please be our light and guide so that we won't be lost or confused. Amen.

17

God's Gift of the Good Shepherd

Materials Needed

For this service you will need copies of the introductory scripture readings for four readers. On your class prayer table place the Bible, a candle, and a picture of the Good Shepherd.

Leader   Jesus is God's greatest gift to us, and he often referred to himself as the Good Shepherd. Shepherds protect, guide, and carefully watch over those given to their care.

Reader One   In scripture we are given an image of God as shepherd.

> *God tends his flock like a shepherd: He gathers the lambs in his arms and carries them close to his heart; he gently leads those that have young (Is 40:11).*

Reader Two   God has always appointed shepherds and prophets to do the work of the kingdom.

> *The Lord said to David, "You will shepherd my people Israel, and you will become their ruler" (2 Sam 5:2).*

Reader Three   When God sent the prophet Nathan to anoint David, David was so grateful that he wrote psalms in praise of God. This is one of his most famous psalms:
> *The Lord is my shepherd, I shall not want. He makes me lie down in green pastures, he leads me beside quiet waters, he restores my*

soul... Even though I walk through the valley
of the shadow of death, I will fear no evil, for
you are with me (Ps 23:1–4).

Reader Four   This is what Jesus says about being a good shepherd:

I am the good shepherd. The good shepherd
lays down his life for the sheep (Jn 10:11).

Leader   Have any of you ever been a caretaker for another person
or a pet? Was it hard work? Did you enjoy it? Did you ever
think of God as taking care of you?

Guided Meditation

Take three deep comfortable breaths... Feel yourself relaxing... Let go of all
your cares and concerns...

•Standing in front of you, in your mind's eye, picture Jesus, the shepherd...
In his arms he holds a white lamb... The lamb is snuggled safely and securely against him...

•Now Jesus sets the lamb down and looks directly at you... He opens his
arms and stretches them out to you... See
yourself moving toward those outstretched arms...

•Picture yourself being picked up as if you
were a small child. Recall how it felt to be
securely held in the arms of a loving parent...
That's how you are being held now...

•Feel the arms of the shepherd holding you...
You are protected by the strongest, bravest
shepherd that ever was or will be...

•Listen now as Jesus tells you how important
you are to him... He says, "You are important to
me, I want you to be safe, I love you."...

•As you rest in the Good Shepherd's arms,
talk to him now in your own words. Tell him
whatever you want him to know about you
right now... Share with him the areas in
your life that need protection and guidance...

Take all the time you need for this… (longer pause)

•When you are ready, move out of the Shepherd's arms, knowing that you are always welcome there…

•Open your eyes and return to the group…

Invite children to discuss this experience if they seem interested in doing so. Or allow them to write about it in their prayer journals.

Closing Prayer

Light the candle on the prayer table and invite one child to hold up the Bible and another the picture of the Good Shepherd as signs that Jesus watches over us always.

Left Side   Jesus, you are the Good Shepherd; you watch over us with love and care.

Right Side   Good Shepherd, we thank you for guiding and protecting us. Help us to be good shepherds to those around us.

All   May we always look to you for our needs. Amen.

18
God's Gift of Animals

Materials Needed

For this service you will need copies of the introductory scripture readings for four readers. On your class prayer table place a candle, the Bible, and miniature statues or drawings of animals found in the Bible. If possible, also have a picture of a dove on your table.

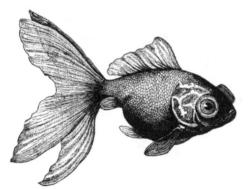

Leader Animals are a special gift from God. They are valued companions; they sometimes give us transportation; they sometimes guard us; and they can be food for us and also provide clothing.

Reader One God created animals and valued them very much.

God made the wild animals according to their kinds, the livestock according to their kinds, and all the creatures that move along the ground according to their kinds. And God saw that it was good (Gen 1:25).

Reader Two Scripture teaches that animals, like humans, need time for rest and renewal, and God respects the needs of all creatures.

The seventh day is a Sabbath to the Lord your God. On it you shall not do any work, neither you, nor your son or daughter... nor your ox, your donkey, or any of your animals... so that they may rest, as you do (Deut 5:14).

Reader Three   Animals can give praise to God just as we can.

The wild animals honor me, the jackals and the owls, because I provide water in the desert and streams in the wasteland... (Is 43:20).

Reader Four   God used the form of an animal to convey a message of love. When Jesus was baptized, we are told of God's response.

The Holy Spirit descended on him in bodily form like a dove. And a voice came from heaven: "You are my Son, whom I love; with you I am well pleased" (Lk 3:22).

Leader   One by one, I invite you to call out the name of an animal you have known and cared for. Or perhaps just one you admire. (After all have had a turn, continue.) Now think for a moment about the wonder of this animal and of all the animals created by God.

Guided Meditation

Close your eyes... Take three deep comfortable breaths... Feel yourself relaxing, going into a deep healthy level of mind...

• Imagine that you hear the gentle cooing of a bird... or the flap of wings of a bird in flight... Imagine next that a large white dove-like bird is landing near you, looking at you...

• The white bird is walking toward you... You sense that it is your friend... it has been sent by God... The bird lifts one wing and holds it up... You are being invited to come under the wing...

•Can you make yourself small enough to accept this invitation and move yourself under this soft white wing?…

•In your mind's eye, see yourself moving closer to the bird… See yourself resting snugly under its wing…

•Being there is like being under a protective canopy… You understand that this is what it's like to be in God's care… You feel safe and loved there…

•You hear the bird cooing softly as if speaking words of comfort just for you… This gives you a feeling of peace.

•With the song of this loving bird in your ears, talk to God now about feeling safe and happy… Ask God to watch over you always, and tell God about your problems or worries… Take as much time as you need for this…(longer pause)

•Sensing that you are at peace, the bird raises its wing and you come from under it. The bird looks at you lovingly, as if to say, "You can rest in God always."

•When you are ready, return to your place in the room and open your eyes.

Invite children to discuss this experience if they choose. Or, allow them to write about it in their prayer journals.

Closing Prayer

Light the candle on the prayer table and invite children to hold up the animal figures, pictures, etc., as reminders of God's gift of animals.

Right Side   Generous God, thank you for the song of birds, and for animals who are our companions and protectors.

Left Side   May we always remember that everything you have created is good.

All   Help us to be grateful for animals and to treat them with love and care. Amen.

19
God's Gift of Earth

Materials Needed

For this service you will need copies of the introductory scripture readings for four readers. On your class prayer table place a candle, a Bible, the globe of the world, one small stone for each participant, and a representation of the sun, clouds, or some heavenly body.

Leader   Earth, the planet on which we live, is God's gift to us. The heavens, the region surrounding Earth, including the clouds, the sky, the sun, moon, and stars are also great gifts.

Reader One   The Bible begins this way:

> *In the beginning God created the heavens and the earth. God called the dry ground "land," and the gathered waters God called "seas." And God saw that it was good (Gen 1:1, 1:10).*

Reader Two   Jesus spoke often of Heaven and Earth. He said that Earth was a temporary place.

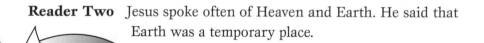

> *Do not store up for yourselves treasures on earth, where moth and rust destroy, and where thieves break in and steal. But store up for yourselves treasures in heaven (Mt 6:19–20).*

Reader Three   After his death, Jesus sent his Holy Spirit to help us be faithful followers here on Earth.

> *You will receive power when the Holy Spirit comes upon you; and you will be my witnesses in Jerusalem, and in all Judea and Samaria, and to the ends of the earth (Acts 1:8).*

Reader Four   Jesus also taught that here on Earth we will not always be treated with justice, but if we are faithful followers, we will receive the reward of Heaven.

Leader   I invite you now to come up to our prayer table and take a stone, which represents Earth. Keep this close to you as we pray the guided meditation.

Guided Meditation

Close your eyes... Take three deep comfortable breaths and feel yourself relaxing... You are now going into a deeper and deeper level of mind... God often communicates from such a quiet place in your mind...

•Imagine yourself entering a great, huge, stone church, built somewhere in an ancient city... As you enter the high-ceilinged hallway you see a stairway at the end of the hall...

•Walk toward the stairway and slowly climb the steps...

•As you climb, notice that there are drawings carved into the huge stones along the wall... These stones were cut and carved out of a deep pit in the earth, yet now they are part of a church where people come to worship God...

•You notice now that these stone carvings tell the story of God's love for us... The story begins with Adam and Eve in the garden, but you also see Abraham and Sarah, Moses and Joshua, David and the prophets...

•As you move up the stairs to the next landing, you see a carving of Mary being told by an angel that she will give birth to the long-awaited Messiah... Notice the look on Mary's face...

•Now move up the stairs again until you come to the next stone carving... This one shows a field of shepherds near a stable, angels are singing... Listen... Can you hear them?...

•You pass many more carvings until you see one with Jesus holding high a cup... His friends are around a table with him... He looks sad... Try to remember why...

•The next carving is of an empty tomb... A golden glow surrounds it... Try to remember why this might be so...

•When you look around you, you realize that you have reached the top of the stairway... There is a door at the end of the hall... Light is coming from it...

•Push the door open now... Jesus is standing there, he motions for you to enter the room... Talk to him now about the carvings you saw or about whatever is in your heart... Stay with Jesus this way for a while... (longer pause)

•When you are ready, open your eyes and return to the group...

Invite children to discuss this experience if they seem interested in doing so. Or allow them to write about it in their prayer journals.

Closing Prayer

Light the candle on the prayer table and invite children to hold up their stones as they pray after you.

Leader Heavenly Father, loving creator,
we thank you for all your gifts.
Thank you for the sky and clouds,
for waterways and deserts,
for mountains and valleys,
for the moon and the stars.
Thank you for the gift of Earth. Amen.

20

God's Gift of Talents

Materials Needed

For this service you will need copies of the introductory scripture readings for the four readers. On your class prayer table place a candle, a Bible, and a list of talents the children in your class possess—as you have determined them. Be sure to name at least one talent for each child.

Leader God has given all of us many talents, even if we haven't yet recognized them.
Our talents include: being a friend, riding a bike, listening well, playing an instrument, being athletic, singing a song, doing nice things, painting a picture, being able to read well, and many, many more.

Reader One Abraham and Sarah had a special talent called hospitality. They welcomed strangers into their home and shared their food. Once they entertained angels without even knowing it (Gen 18:1–8).

Reader Two In the Bible story of David and Goliath, David was only a boy, but he was very intelligent. The giant laughed at David's youth and small size. But David defeated Goliath because he had the talent of good sense (1 Sam 17:45–49).

Reader Three   St. Paul advised the early Christians to praise and thank God often for all their gifts and talents. In one of his letters he praised the hard work of two Christians in these words:

> *I rejoice at the hard work they have done.*
> *Their good example has refreshed my spirit*
> *and I thank them for this (1 Cor 16:13–18).*

Reader Four   In his prayer, Jesus often thanked God. We, too, should say thank you to God for our many gifts and talents. We should never take them for granted.

Leader   I invite each of you to take a moment now to think of one special talent you have for which you would like to thank God. *(pause)* Let me share with you my list of some of your talents. *Name the child and then the talent, as on your list.* Remember these as we enter our guided meditation.

Guided Meditation

Relax and close your eyes… Take three deep, comfortable breaths and feel your troubles flowing away…

•Picture a bright light, a light as bright as the sun… God made the light and saw that it was good.

•Now look at your hands and see God's light glowing from them… Admire these glowing hands that God has given you… As you look at them, think of a project that you want to complete or an activity you want to do using your hands… Thank God that your hands can do these things…

•Picture yourself in your mind's eye, working on this project or activity… Take all the time you need to work on this… See God's golden light surrounding your hands as you work… (longer pause)

•Feel a sense of pride and joy filling you as you work… Allow your mind and spirit to be in tune with God's work of creation as you "create" your project or activity…

•Imagine now that your project is completed as perfectly as you can make it at this time… Feel the golden light of God expanding around you… Relax and enjoy the light… Spend time now talking to God about what you hope to achieve in the future or about whatever is in your heart.

•When you are ready, open your eyes and return to the group.

Invite children to discuss this experience if they seem interested in doing so. Or allow them to write about it in their prayer journals.

Closing Prayer

Light the candle on the prayer table and invite one of the children to hold up your list of talents—as a sign that God has given all of us talents.

Left Side   Loving God, God of light, we thank you for all the gifts and talents you have given us. Thank you especially for our hands that can make and do things.

Right Side   May our projects and activities always please you and may we always walk in your light.

All   May we always recognize and be happy about the gifts and talents of others. Amen.

21
God's Gift of Forgiveness

Materials Needed

For this service you will need copies of the introductory scripture reading for four readers. On the class prayer table place a candle, a Bible, and a crucifix or a large picture of Jesus on the cross.

Leader   God gives us the gift of forgiveness. But forgiveness is also a gift we can give to others. This involves letting go of resentment, revenge, or the desire to punish someone for hurting us. God has given the gift of forgiveness to all of us.

Reader One   The Bible teaches that God is a loving and forgiving God who strengthens us to obey the commandments.

> *You shall not put the Lord your God to the test, but keep the commandments of the Lord, your God. Do what is right and good in the sight of the Lord (Deut 6:16–17).*

Reader Two   Scripture instructs us to solve our problems with others through forgiveness.

My brothers and sisters, bear with one another and forgive one another. If you have a grievance with one another, forgive as the Lord has forgiven you (Col 3:13).

Reader Three   Jesus spoke often of forgiveness. He said,

For if you forgive others when they sin against you, your heavenly Father will also forgive you (Mt 6:14).

Reader Four   Jesus claimed the authority only God has. He once said:

"Which is easier to say to the paralytic, 'Your sins are forgiven,' or to say, 'Get up, take your mat and walk'?

But that you may know that the Son of Man has authority on earth to forgive sins…. He said to the paralytic, "I tell you, get up, take your mat and go home."

He got up, took his mat and walked out in full view of them all. This amazed everyone and they praised God, saying, "We have never seen anything like this!" (Mk 2:9–12).

Leader   I invite you to come forward one by one and examine the crucifix (or the picture of Jesus on the cross) on our prayer table. As you look at it, imagine the pain and rejection Jesus felt. Does anyone remember the words Jesus said about forgiveness before he died? (After this short discussion continue as below.)

Guided Meditation

Close your eyes… Take three deep comfortable breaths and feel yourself relaxing… Let go of all your worries and troubles…

•Imagine that you are sitting alone in a dark movie theater. The screen lights up and your name begins to roll across it… After your name, like the title of a film, the words Remember to Forgive blaze across the screen…

•Now recall a time when someone hurt you deeply by forgetting about you… Imagine that this memory is going from your mind up to the screen.

See the memory happening on the screen in front of you…

•How old were you?… How were you dressed?… Who is with you in this scene on the screen?…

•Why were you forgotten?… What else was going on?… Why did it bother you so much?… Do you understand anything now that you didn't understand when the hurt happened?…

•As you watch this event, ask yourself: can I forgive the one who hurt me?… Can I let go of the anger or resentment that I feel for that person?…

•Take another deep comfortable breath and hold it for a few seconds… Then ask Jesus to help you learn how to forgive. Tell him in your own words how you feel about the things people have done to you…

•Then listen to what Jesus wants to say to you. Imagine that you can feel the resentment going out of you as he speaks to you…

•Ponder this a while and know that you can talk to Jesus any time you wish. He is always ready to listen. He will strengthen you to forgive.

•When you are ready, open your eyes and return to the group…

Invite the children to share their reactions to this experience or to write about it in their prayer journals.

Closing Prayer

Light the candle on the prayer table. Invite one of the children to hold up the crucifix (or picture) as a sign that Jesus forgives us and we can forgive others.

Left Side	Dear kind and forgiving Jesus, you were hurt so badly by those who should have loved you. We, too, have been hurt and rejected.
Right Side	Help us to be forgiving. Help us to learn that when we forgive others we release ourselves from pain and trouble.
All	Thank you for all the times you have forgiven us. Amen.

OLD RESENTMENTS

22

God's Gift of Prayer

Materials Needed

For this service you will need copies of the introductory scripture readings for four readers. On you class prayer table place a candle, the Bible, and a picture or drawing of praying hands.

Leader   God gives us the gift of prayer, which is the ability to talk to God in the quiet of our own hearts as well as with others. When we pray, we raise our hearts and minds to God in praise, in petition, in thanksgiving, and in sorrow for our weakness and sins.

Reader One   Scripture teaches that God always communicates with us first.

> *Then the man and his wife heard the sound of the Lord God walking in the garden in the cool of the day, and they hid from the Lord God among the trees of the garden. But the Lord God called to them, "Where are you?" (Gen 3:8–9).*

Reader Two   The Bible also teaches that God calls each one of us into a personal relationship. One of the psalms says it this way:

> *But you are a shield around me, O Lord; you bestow glory on me and lift up my head. To you I cry aloud, and you answer me from your holy hill (Ps 3:3–5).*

Reader Three   In the New Testament, Jesus says this about prayer:

> *This, then, is how you should pray: "Our Father in heaven, hallowed be your name, your kingdom come, your will be done on earth as it is in heaven" (Mt 6:9–10).*

Reader Four   Jesus also teaches us to be bold in prayer.

> *Therefore I tell you, whatever you ask for in prayer, believe that you have received it, and it will be yours (Mk 11:24).*

Now invite children to share some of the ways that they pray. Ask for examples of times God has communicated with them—if they wish to share them. (After sharing, continue as below.)

Guided Meditation

Close your eyes... Take three deep comfortable breaths... and feel yourself going into a relaxed state of mind... a place of peace, safety, and joy...

•Picture yourself walking through a cloud into the open arms of God the Father... Feel the Father picking you up and holding you gently in his arms... God whispers to you, "I think you are special"... How do you feel about this?...

•Whisper to God in return, "I think you are very special, too, God"... Now imagine that God is lifting you high, high enough so you can see all of Earth... Can you see the water swirling around?... The green trees and plants?...

•Whisper to God, "I thank you for Earth, and the water, and the wind, and all that you have made."...

•Picture God now carrying you over a cloud...Can you feel the clean moist air surrounding the cloud?... An airplane glides away at a safe distance from you...

•Whisper to God, "Only you could have created such wonderful things."

•Remember now the many different ways that you usually pray to God… At home with your family?… At Mass?… At school?… When you are afraid?… When you are happy or grateful?… Stay with these special prayer memories for a few minutes…

•Now imagine that God is slowly carrying you back to Earth… Before God puts you down he whispers, "I love you."… You whisper in return, "I love you, too."…

•When you are ready open your eyes and return to the group…

Invite the children to discuss this experience if they seem interested in doing so. Or, allow them to write about it in their prayer journals.

Closing Prayer

Light the candle on the prayer table and invite one of the children to hold up the Bible as a sign that God is always with us, listening to our prayers.

Left Side   We love you, dear heavenly Father, who first loved us and who speaks to us often.

Right Side   Help us to always keep our hearts and minds tuned in to you.

All   Remind us to begin and end each day in prayer, and may we always stay close to you as your loving children. Amen.

23
God's Gift of Fire

Materials Needed

On your prayer table you will need a Bible, introductory scripture readings for four readers, a large lighted candle, and enough small candles so that each student will have one (when needed during this the service). Also have a piece of styrofoam, big enough to hold all of the small candles.

Leader   God has given us many gifts of nature, among them the gift of fire. Fire can be useful for keeping us warm and cooking our food. It can offer light and comfort on a cold damp day. Fire can be very beautiful as well.

Reader One   Scripture speaks of fire in connection with the Holy Spirit. John the Baptizer spoke these words,

> *I baptize you with water for repentance. But after me will come one who is more powerful than I, whose sandals I am not fit to carry. He will baptize you with the Holy Spirit and with fire (Mt 3:11).*

Reader Two   St. Peter once said this about fire: *"Just as gold is refined by fire, so our faith is refined by our trials and difficulties. When faith is tested and proved genuine, it reveals Jesus Christ to others" (1 Pet 1:7).*

Reader Three   Controlled fire is often used on camping trips, and friend-ships are often formed around a campfire. Scripture tells us that Jesus had breakfast around a campfire with his friends.

> *When they landed, they saw a fire of burning coals there with fish on it, and some bread. Jesus said to them, "Bring some of the fish you have just caught and I will cook it" (Jn 21:9–10).*

Reader Four   The Bible also tells us that when it is dark, we can still see around firelight. Just as fire reveals hidden things in the dark, God's light will ultimately reveal what is in our hearts. (1 Cor 3:12–13).

Now turn off the lights and invite children to come forward one by one to take a small candle from the table, light it from the large candle, and then place it in the styrofoam container. Comment on how much brighter the room is when the small candles are added to the fire of the large one. If possible, leave the lights off during the Guided Meditation.

Guided Meditation

Find a comfortable position and sit or lie down... Close your eyes... Let go of all your worries and concerns by slightly wiggling your shoulders... Feel them become looser and lighter as though you are shaking off something that had been dragging you down...Take a deep comfortable breath...

•Imagine yourself by the seashore at night... The moon is full... and the wind is blowing... A group of men are in a fishing boat out in the water... Watch them as they struggle to pull in their empty fishing nets...

•You hear the men grumbling loudly... A few of them are yelling out angrily because their nets are empty.

•You notice that it is slowly getting lighter... The sun is rising as though from out of the water... The men are still struggling with their empty fishing nets...

•Suddenly the shining figure of a man appears on shore... He calls to the men in the boat: "Cast your nets off to the starboard side, and you will find something"...

•The men, though still grumbling and arguing, cast their largest net over the starboard side… Fish begin to jump from the sea into the net, so many fish that the net is too full to lift into the boat…

•One of the fishermen, an older man with a gray beard, suddenly shouts, "It is the Lord!" … He drops his hands from the net and jumps wildly into the sea, swimming toward Jesus on shore… The other fishermen follow in the boat, towing the net full of fish… When they land, they see a charcoal fire with fish baking on it… Warm bread is piled nearby… "Bring some of your fish," Jesus says… "Come and eat and warm yourselves by the fire"…

•Then Jesus looks at you. "Come," he says, "Join us"… You find yourself drawn to the fire, wanting to be in the presence of this man…

•After the meal, Jesus asks each one sitting around the fire… "Do you love me?"… Then he looks directly at you… See his smile… See his deep eyes staring into yours… "I love you," he says… "Do you know how much I love you?"…

•As you sit there around that fire, how will you answer this question? Tell Jesus in your own words how you feel about it… (longer pause)

•When you are ready, open your eyes and return to the group…

Invite the children to share their reactions to this prayer experience if they wish, or have them write about it in their prayer journals.

Closing Prayer

Left Side Dear creator God, may we be fed and warmed by the fire that Jesus provides for all who go to him.

Right Side Just as ancient people carried fire to see their way, may we carry the fire of the Holy Spirit to light our way.

All Whenever we see fire, help us to remember the fire of your love for us and show us how to love you in return. Amen.

Before the children leave, blow out the candles and turn on the light. Comment on how candlelight made the room feel special.

24

God's Gift of Rocks

Materials Needed

For this service you will need copies of the scripture readings for four readers. On your prayer table place a candle, the Bible, and a large rock. Ask each child to bring to this service a personal rock, small enough to carry, that he or she considers beautiful.

Leader
Maybe you've never thought about it, but rocks are a special gift from God. Rocks are often mentioned in scripture. They were used long ago to give shelter and to make tools and hunting weapons, and they are still used today for construction purposes and often for decorative purposes like stone walls. Besides, rocks are beautiful just as they are.

Reader One
The Bible tells how God once used a rock when the Israelites were thirsty in the desert.

> *When God's people were wandering in the desert God opened a rock and poured out water (Ex 17:6).*

Reader Two
The great prophet of God, Isaiah said,

> *Trust in the Lord forever, for the Lord is the Rock eternal (Is 26:4).*

Reader Three   The Bible also tells us that a rock was used to seal the tomb of Jesus:

> *Joseph took the body, wrapped it in a clean linen cloth, and placed it in his own new tomb that he had cut out of the rock. He rolled a big stone in front of the entrance to the tomb and went away (Mt 27:59–60).*

Reader Four   In Genesis, the first book of the Bible, God is referred to this way:

> *God is "the shepherd, the Rock of Israel." The Bible also tells us that people who are wise build their houses on rock (Mt 7:24). And, Jesus began his church with the words, "You are Peter, and on this rock I will build my church" (Mt 16:18).*

Leader   I invite all of you to now pick up your personal rock. Hold it in your hand and become familiar with how it feels. Experience the strength and beauty of your rock. Keep it near you as I guide you through the following meditation.

Guided Meditation

Take a moment or two to get into a comfortable position. Relax and close your eyes.... Take three deep comfortable breaths and feel yourself relaxing more and more...

•Picture Jesus, strong and true, standing on a mountain road... Behind him is a huge reddish colored rock... He begins to climb a short mountain trail, and he is beckoning for you to follow him... Imagine yourself climbing up behind him.

•At the top Jesus finds a flat place to sit... He is smiling at you, motioning for you to join him...

•Feel the warm air surrounding you... Listen to the birds singing... Relax and enjoy the view...

•Notice now that Jesus is looking at you, smiling... He has a question for you. He asks, "Will you help me to spread the gospel?"

•Spend a few minutes discussing this with Jesus... Why has he chosen you? What can you do to spread the gospel? What gifts and talents does he think you have?

•Then discuss with Jesus how you feel about the gospel... How does it guide you and help you? Talk to Jesus about this in your own words.

•Stay with this conversation until you are satisfied that Jesus understands your feelings for now... Know that you are completely accepted by him and that he will always guide and strengthen you. He is your rock....

•Now Jesus is getting up from the rock... He is going to move on, but he reminds you that he travels with you always...

•Think about this as you picture Jesus walking off. When you are ready, open your eyes and return to the group.

Invite the children to share this experience if they choose. Or have them write about it in their prayer journals. Then recite the Closing Prayer together.

Closing Prayer
Light the candle on the prayer table. Invite all the children to bring their rock and place it close to the larger rock which is the symbol of Jesus.

Left Side	Dear Jesus, we give thanks that you are our Rock, our reason to believe. You are our strength and our weapon against the enemy.
Right Side	Please be our foundation. We want you to be the building block in our lives.
All	We want to work with you to spread your gospel and to be "rocks" for others in your name. Amen.

25

God's Gift of Mary

Materials Needed

For this service you will need copies of the introductory scripture readings for four readers. On the class prayer table place a candle, the Bible, and a statue or picture of Mary, the mother of Jesus and our mother and model.

Leader   The Blessed Mother of Jesus is the greatest example of motherhood ever known. She loved, protected, nourished, supported, encouraged, and taught Jesus. On the cross Jesus gave his mother to us so we may all benefit from her love.

Reader One   When the Angel Gabriel asked Mary if she would be the mother of the savior, Mary responded,

> *"I am the Lord's servant, may it be done to me as you have said" (Lk 1:38).*

Reader Two   When Jesus was twelve years old, he stayed behind after the family had visited the Temple. Just as any parent whose child is missing, Mary let Jesus know she was very concerned.

> *When his parents saw him, they were astonished. His mother said to him, "Son, why*

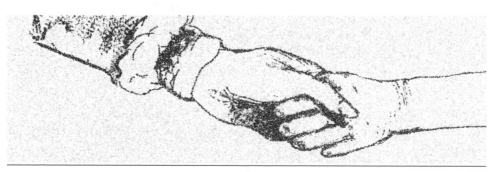

have you treated us like this? Your father and I have been anxiously searching for you" (Lk 2:48).

Reader Three   When Jesus grew up, Mary stayed close. She was responsible for his first public miracle.

On the third day a wedding took place at Cana in Galilee. Jesus' mother was there, and Jesus and his disciples had also been invited to the wedding. When the wine was gone, Jesus' mother said to him, "They have no more wine."

"Mother, why do you involve me?" Jesus replied. "My time has not yet come." His mother said to the servants, "Do whatever he tells you" (Jn 2:1–5).

Reader Four   As Jesus died, Mary stood at the foot of the cross, faithful as ever. At that time Jesus gave his mother to John and thus to all of us.

When Jesus saw his mother there, and the disciple whom he loved standing nearby, he said to his mother, "Dear woman, here is your son," and to the disciple, "Here is your mother." From that time on, this disciple took her into his home (Jn 19:26–27).

Leader   Take a few minutes and discuss with children the characteristics of a good mother. Ask them to share some of the good qualities of their own mothers, grandmothers, and caregivers. (After a few minutes continue as below.)

Guided Meditation

Close your eyes and take several deep breaths… Feel yourself relaxing more and more, and watch your cares and worries drift away…

•Now imagine that a huge white cloud is hovering above you… As you gaze at the cloud take three more deep breaths… The cloud is moving in closer to you… The cloud has surrounded you completely and it feels very safe and comfortable…

•Imagine that in this cloud you meet Mary, the mother of Jesus… See her smile… Notice her caring eyes gazing at you… Feel her hand reaching out to take yours…

•Holding her hand, walk together to the edge of the cloud where you can see a silky white curtain...

•Mary pulls open the curtain... and there is a long corridor behind it... With Mary still holding your hand, begin to walk down the corridor...

•After a short distance, Mary stops and points to a scene taking place in a cloud at the side of the corridor... It is you as a baby... You are laughing, being held lovingly... Enjoy this scene for a while...

•Mary gently tugs at you and you move on... Soon you and Mary stop again to view a happy scene of you and your mother or father on your way to school... Can you remember that day?... Can you remember being glad your parent was with you?...

•You are moving on now, down the corridor... This time when Mary stops you see yourself as you are now... Some of your friends are there... Are your parents in this scene?... Even if not, Mary reminds you that Jesus is always with you... She asks you if the way you live now reflects the presence of Jesus... Talk to Mary about this for a few minutes...

•At the end of the corridor, Mary lets go of your hand. She smiles at you... She is leaving now, disappearing into a cloud...

•In your mind and spirit, can you believe that Jesus will come to help you whenever you need him?... Do you believe Mary's words?... How did it feel to be led by Jesus' mother?...

•Take another deep breath... Relax... And when you are ready return to the group...

Invite the children to discuss this experience if they seem interested in doing so. Or allow them to write about it in their prayer journals.

Closing Prayer

Light the candle on the prayer table and invite one of the children to hold up Mary's picture or statue as a sign that Mary points the way to Jesus.

Left Side	Dear God, thank you for giving us Jesus and his mother Mary.
Right Side	Help us to be good children for our parents and caregivers and to love them as Jesus loved Mary.
All	We believe that Jesus is always with us, loving and guiding us. Thank you for this great gift. Amen.

Of Related Interest ...

Children, Imagination and Prayer
Creative Techniques for Middle Grade Students
Pat Egan Dexter
The author gives step-by-step directions for bringing students to a new and meditative experience of prayer.
0-89622-565-8, 80 pp, $7.95 (order C-70)

Dear Jesus, Dear Child
Guided Meditations for Young Children
Deborah Roslak and Linda Orber
Joys, fears and needs of primary-grade children are focused on here in an easy-to-use and inviting format.
0-89622-508-9, 96 pp, $9.95 (order B-36)

Prayer Services for Young Adolescents
Gwen Costello
Common concerns of 10-14 year-olds are addressed through group and private prayer and Scripture reflections. Particularly appealing is the guided meditation in each service.
0-89622-597-6, 80 pp. $9.95 (order M-02)

Teen Assemblies, Retreats and Prayer Services
Greg Dues
The 20 prayer experiences found in this book are straight-forward, with a minimum amount of preparation time needed.
0-89622-561-5, 96 pp, $9.95 (order C-38)

Teenagers Come and Pray!
Michael D. Ausperk
26 practical and pertinent prayer services for contemporary teens.
0-89622-642-5, 112 pp, $12.95 (order M-35)

Teen Prayer Services
20 Themes for Reflection
Kevin Regan
Services focus on issues important to teens. Great for retreats, special sessions and regular classes.
0-89622-520-8, 80 pp, $9.95 (order C-75)

20 More Teen Prayer Services
Kevin Regan
Each prayer service contains a mini-lesson, and includes suggested times for use, a list of materials needed, an introduction, shared experience and the prayer service.
0-89622-605-0, 112 p, $9.95 (order M-04)

Seasonal Prayer Services for Teenagers
Greg Dues
These 16 prayer services help teenagers understand the seasonal themes found in the holidays, the church year and the civic year.
0-89622-473-2, 80 pp, $9.95 (order C-53)

Available at religious bookstores or from:

TWENTY-THIRD PUBLICATIONS
XXIII P.O. Box 180 • Mystic, CT 06355 • 1-800-321-0411